ORNAMENT
AND
DESIGN
OF THE
ALHAMBRA

OWEN JONES

DOVER PUBLICATIONS, INC.
MINEOLA, NEW YORK

Bibliographical Note

This Dover edition, first published in 2008, is a new selection of color plates from *The Alhambra: Being a Brief Record of the Arabian Conquest of the Peninsula with a Particular Account of the Mohammedan Architecture and Decoration,* by Albert F. Calvert, originally published by John Lane, The Bodley Head, London and John Lane Company, New York, in 1906.

DOVER *Pictorial Archive* SERIES

Library of Congress Cataloging-in-Publication Data

Jones, Owen.
    Ornament and design of the Alhambra / Owen Jones.
        p. cm.
    "This Dover edition, first published in 2008, is a new selection of color plates from The Alhambra: being a brief record of the Arabian conquest of the peninsula with a particular account of the Mohammedan architecture and decoration, by Albert F. Calvert, originally published by John Lane, The Bodley Head, London, and John Lane Company, New York, in 1906."
    ISBN-13: 978-0-486-46524-1
    ISBN-10: 0-486-46524-1
    1. Alhambra (Granada, Spain). 2. Decoration and ornament, Islamic—Spain—Granada. 3. Architecture, Islamic—Spain—Granada. I. Calvert, Albert Frederick, 1872–1946. Alhambra. Selections. II. Title.

NA387.C22 2008
728.8'2094682—dc22

                                                    2007046749

Manufactured in the United States of America
Dover Publications, Inc., 31 East 2nd Street, Mineola, N.Y. 11501

NOTE

The Alhambra is a magnificent Moorish palace overlooking Granada, Spain. The first reference to this fortress dates back to the ninth century, but it wasn't until the thirteenth century that it became an official royal residence. The Alhambra is a rare architectural jewel and is one of the most photographed places in the world.

Welsh architect Owen Jones (1809–1874) was responsible for producing the first chromolithographic book in Britain, his subject—the Alhambra. "We find in the Alhambra the speaking art of the Egyptians, the natural grace and refinement of the Greeks, the geometrical combinations of the Romans, the Byzantines, and the Arabs," says Jones about the beauty of this timeless treasure. He became involved with doing a detailed survey of the Alhambra with French architect Jules Goury (1803–1834), producing many drawings and paintings of the interior and exterior of the palace. Unfortunately, Goury died before the research was complete. Jones was determined to publish these fantastic drawings, so he set up his own publishing means and produced the collection at his own expense in order to share these magnificent illustrations with the world. This book showcases a selection of images that were originally from Jones's amazing collection.

Ornament in panels on the walls; Hall of the Ambassadors.

Soffit of an arch; Court of the Fish Pond.

Ornament over doorway at the entrance; Court of the Lions.

Ornament in doorway at the entrance to the ventana; Hall of the Two Sisters.

4

Ornament on the side of windows, upper story; Hall of the Two Sisters.

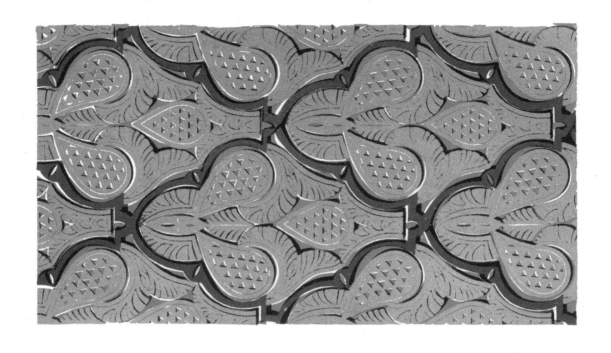

Ornament in spandrels of arches; Hall of the Abencerrages.

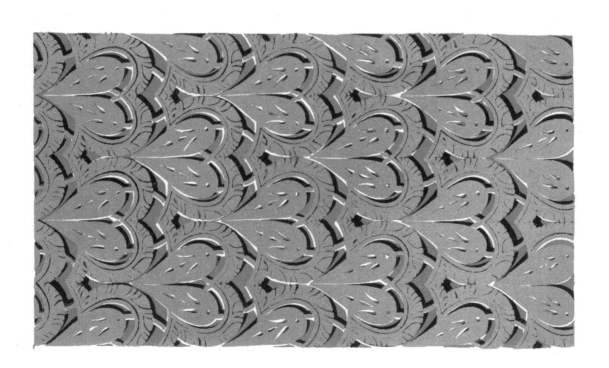

Ornament in spandrels of arches; Hall of the Two Sisters.

Small panel in jamb of a window; Hall of the Two Sisters.

Ornaments in panels; Hall of the Ambassadors.

8

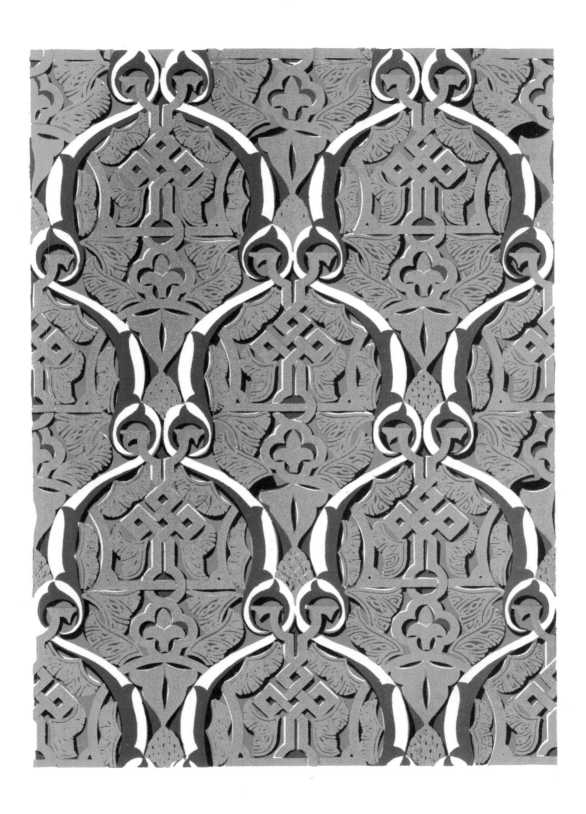

Ornaments in panels; Court of the Mosque.

Ornament over arches at the entrance to the Court of the Lions.

Ornament on the walls; Hall of the Abencerrages.

Ornament in panels on the walls; Court of the Mosque.

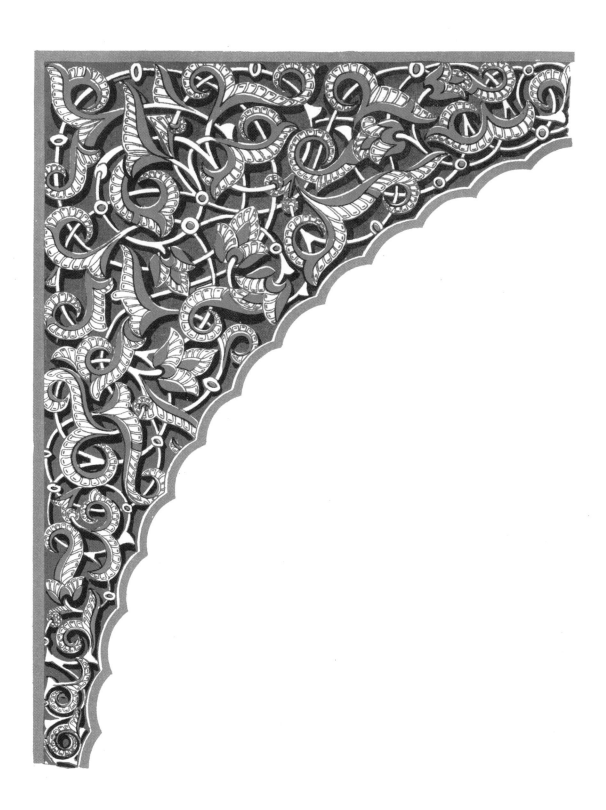

Spandrel of an arch of window; Hall of the Ambassadors.

Brackets supporting ceiling of the portico; Court of the Lions.

Small panel in jamb of a window; Hall of the Ambassadors.

Small panel in jamb of a window; Hall of the Ambassadors.

Panel in the upper chamber of the House of Sanchez.

Soffit of great arch at the entrance of the Court of the Fish Pond.

Spandrel from niche of doorway at the entrance of the Hall of the Ambassadors,
from the Sala de la Barca.

Lintel of a doorway; Court of the Mosque.

20

Capital of columns; Court of the Lions.

Capital of columns; Court of the Lions.

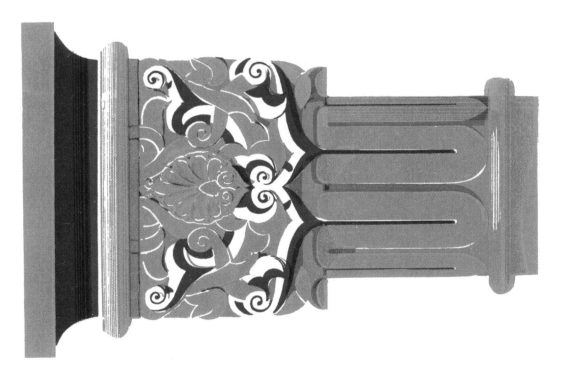

Capital of columns; Court of the Fish Pond.

23

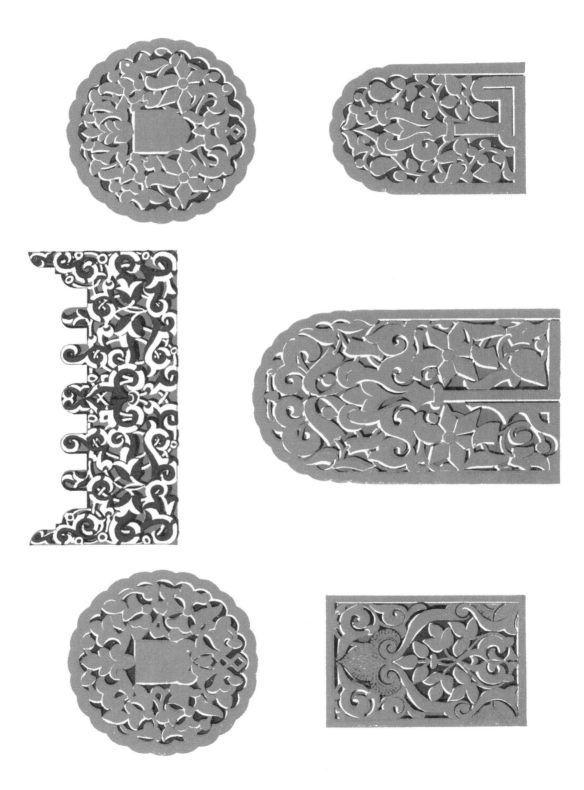

Ornament on the walls of the windows of "Lindaraja's" Balcony.

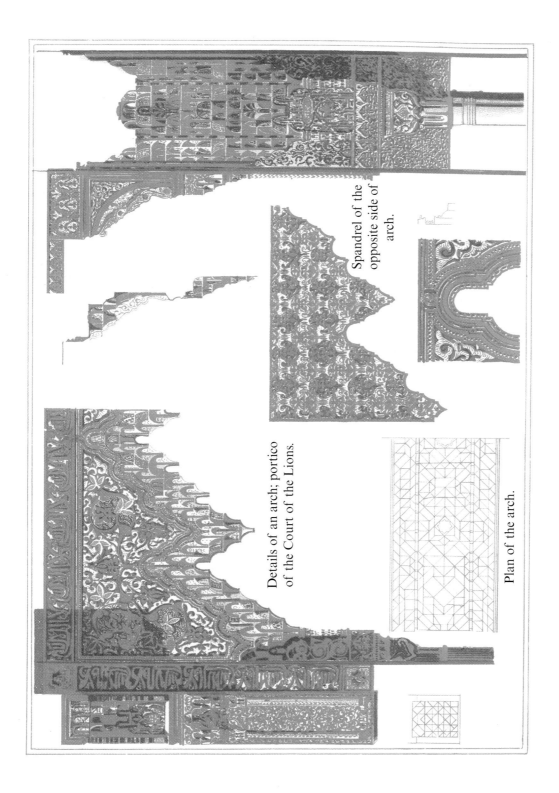

Spandrel of the opposite side of arch.

Details of an arch; portico of the Court of the Lions.

Plan of the arch.

Court of the Lions.

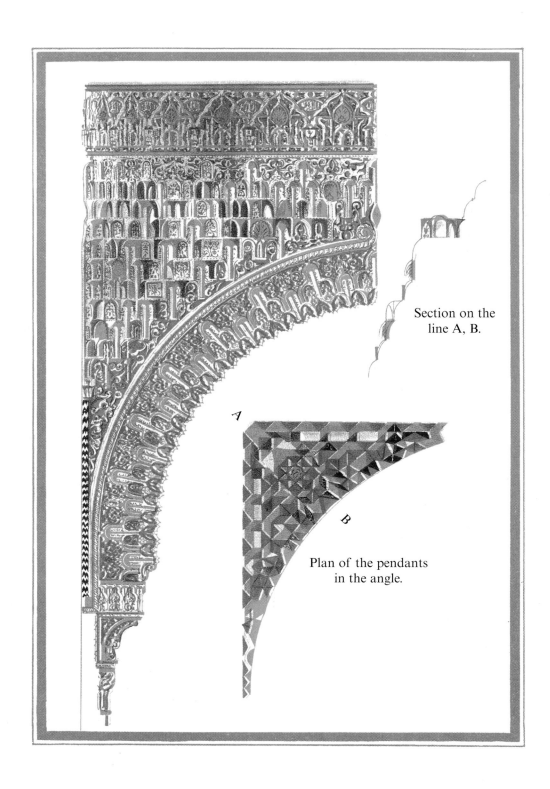

Section on the
line A, B.

Plan of the pendants
in the angle.

Details of the great arches in the Hall of the Bark.

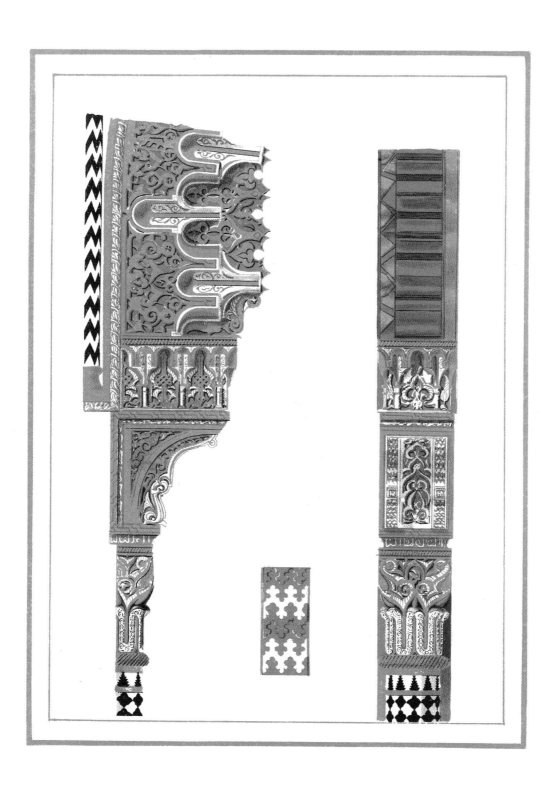

Details of the great arches.

1. Hall of the Ambassadors.
2. Court of the Fish Pond.

3. Hall of the Bark
4. Hall of the Two Sisters.

28

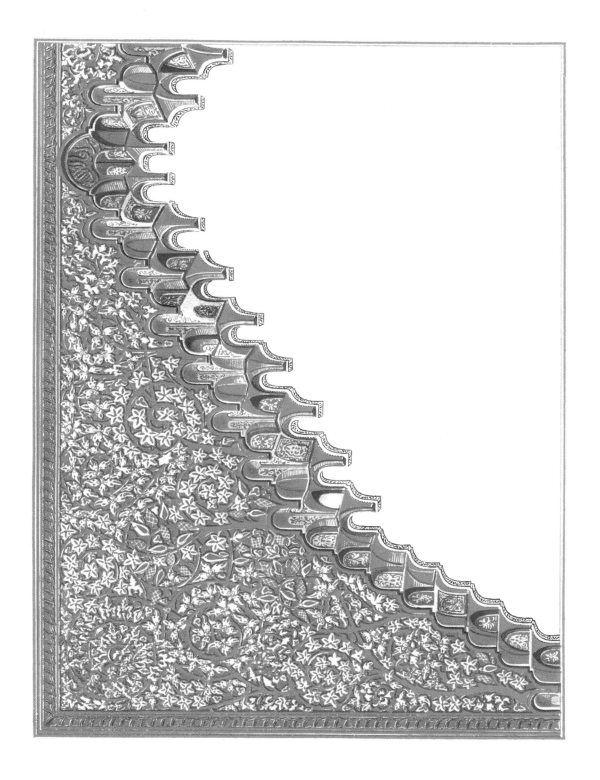

Detail of an arch; Court of the Fish Pond.

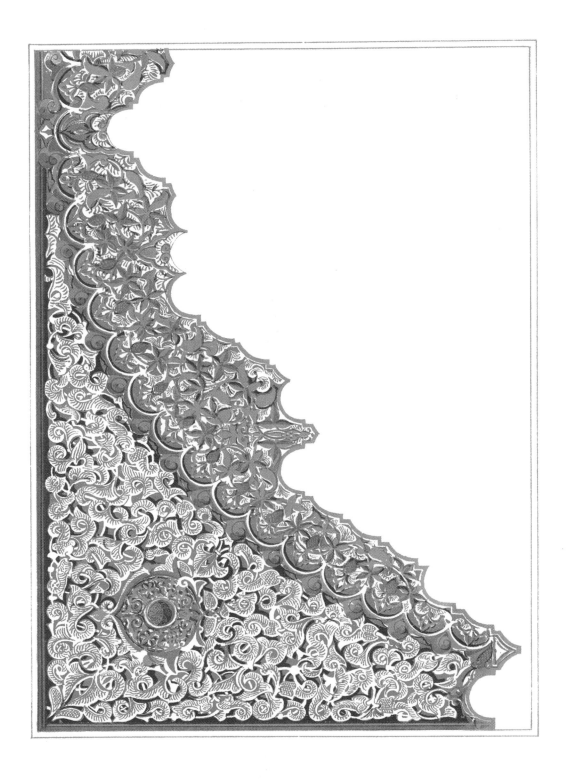

Detail of an arch; portico of the Court of the Lions.

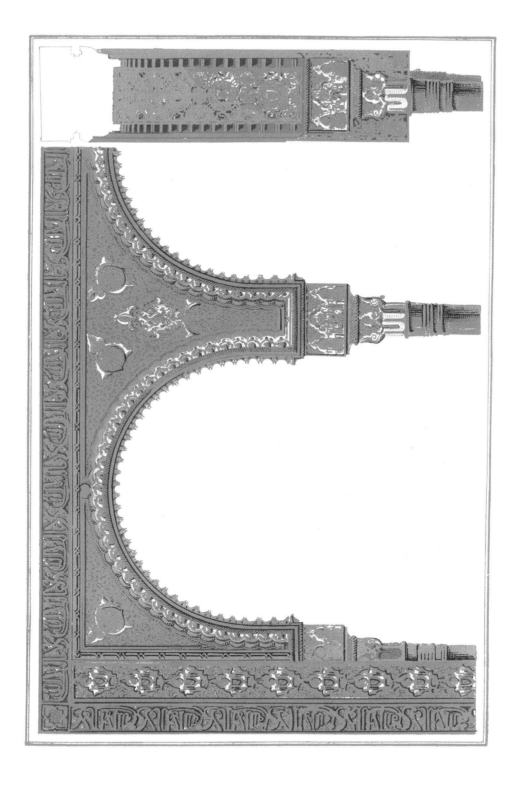

Details of the arches; Hall of the Abencerrages.

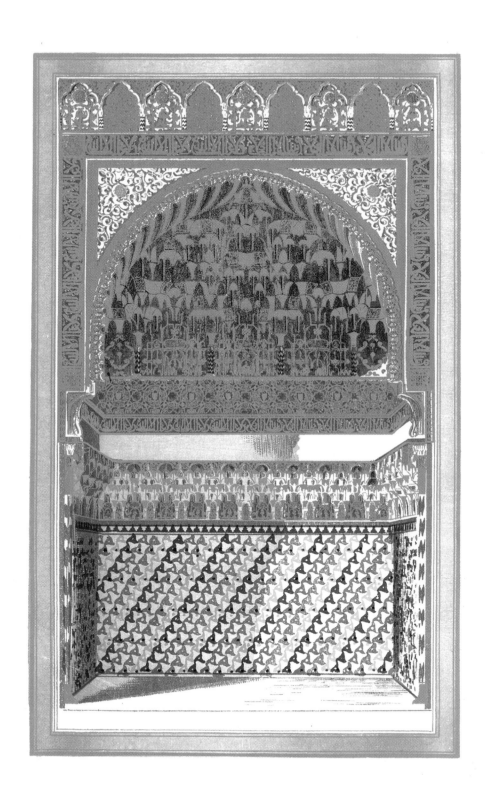

Divan; Court of the Fish Pond.

Windows in the alcove; Hall of the Two Sisters.

Height of Vase 4 ft. 5 in.   Diameter 2 ft. 11 in.

The vase.

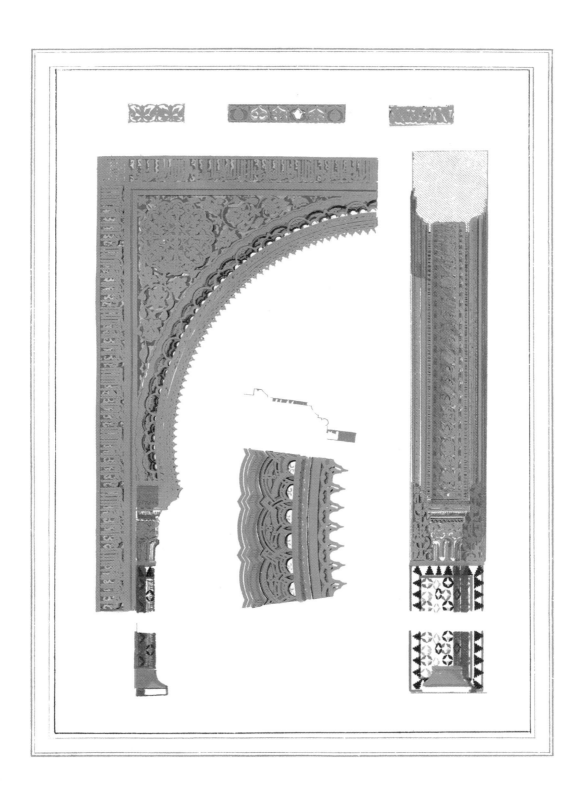

Details of one of the arches; Hall of Justice.

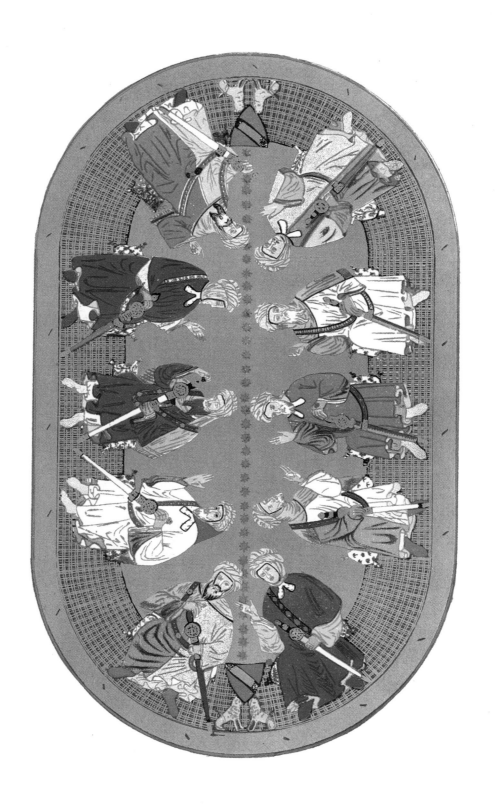

Center painting on the ceiling; Hall of Justice.

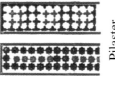

Pilaster.

Center ornament of the window.

Dado.

Dado.

Pilaster.

Mosaic dado in center window on the north side; Hall of the Ambassadors.

Mosaic dados on pillars between the windows; Hall of the Ambassadors.

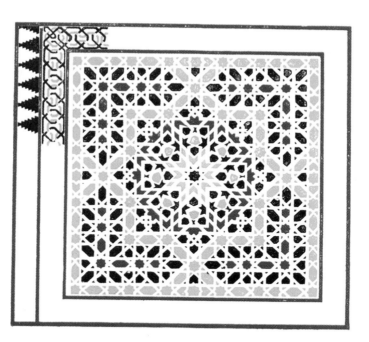

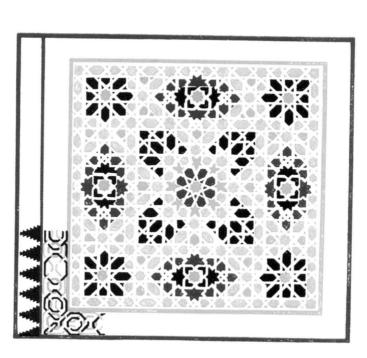

Mosaic dados on pillars between the windows; Hall of the Ambassadors.

39

Pilaster.

Dado.

Dado.

Lining of one of
the columns.

Dado.

Mosaics in the Hall of the Two Sisters.

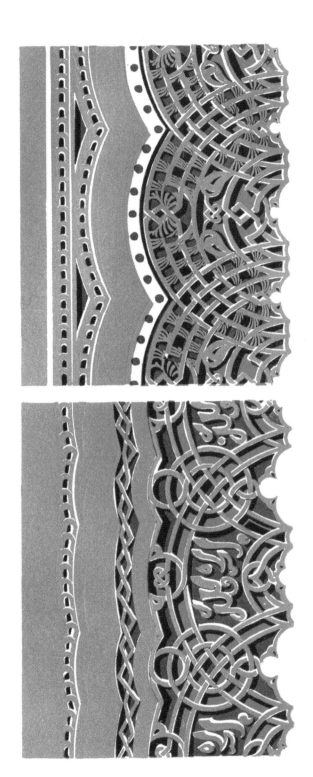

Borders of the arches.

Pavement of the Hall of the Baths.

Mosaic dado round the internal walls of the mosque.

Mosaics from the mosque and the Hall of the Baths.

42

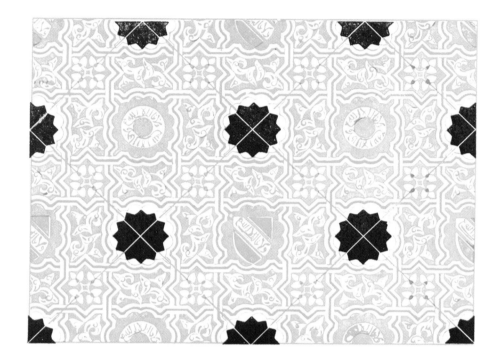

Painted tiles *(azulejos)*.

Floor of one of the alcoves; Hall of Justice (center).

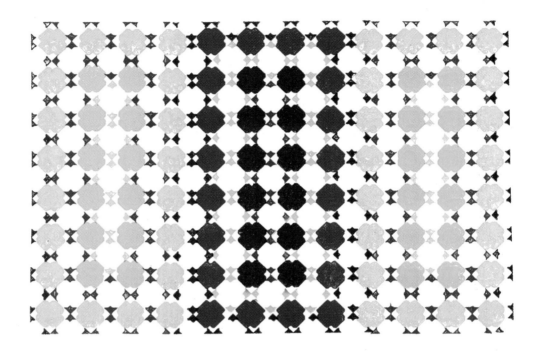

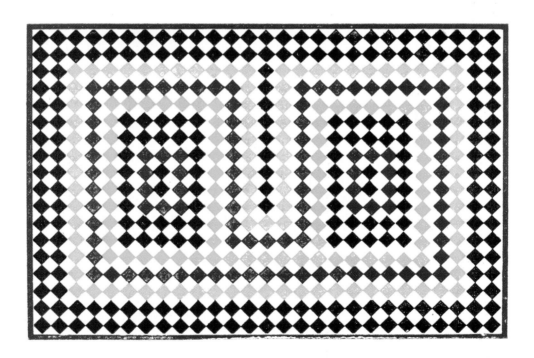

Mosaics in the baths.

Mosaic from the portico of the Generalife.

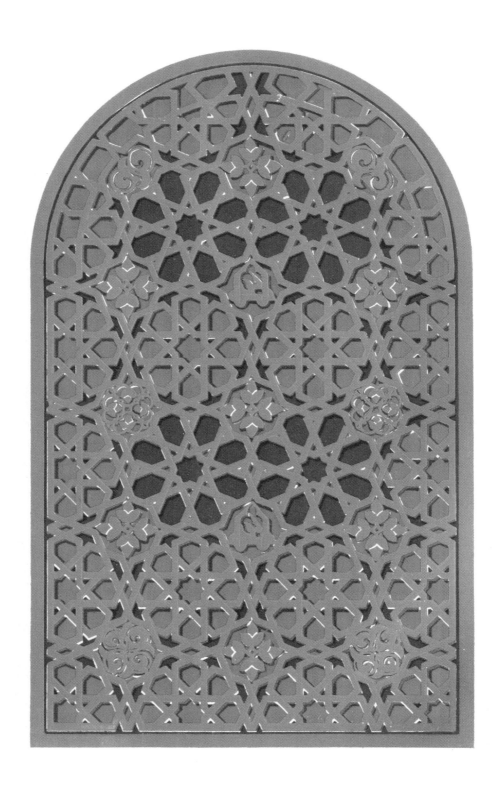

Blank window; Hall of the Bark.

Soffit of arch; entrance of the Hall of the Abencerrages.

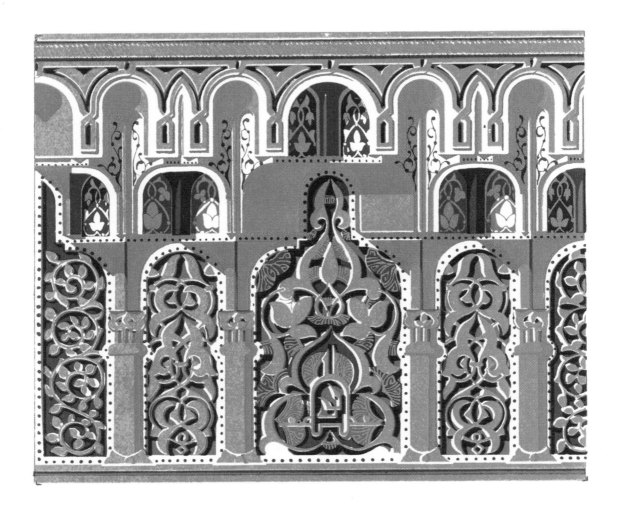

Cornice at springing of arch of doorway at the entrance of the ventana; Hall of the Two Sisters.

Ornament in panels on the wall; Hall of the Ambassadors.

Border of arches.

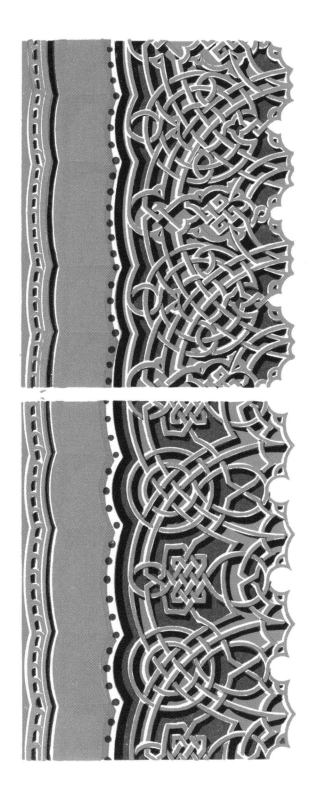

Borders of arches.

Ornaments painted on the pendants; Hall of the Bark.

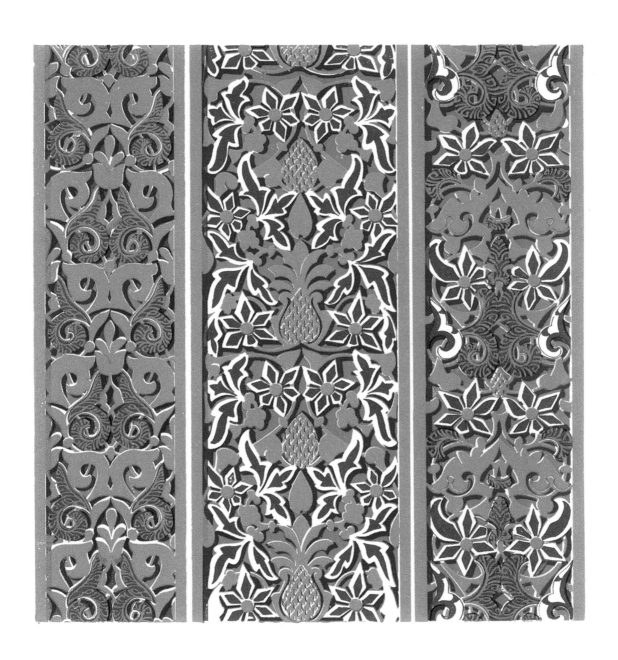

Bands, sides of arches; Court of the Lions.

Bands, sides of arches; Court of the Lions.

Ornaments on panels; Hall of the Ambassadors.

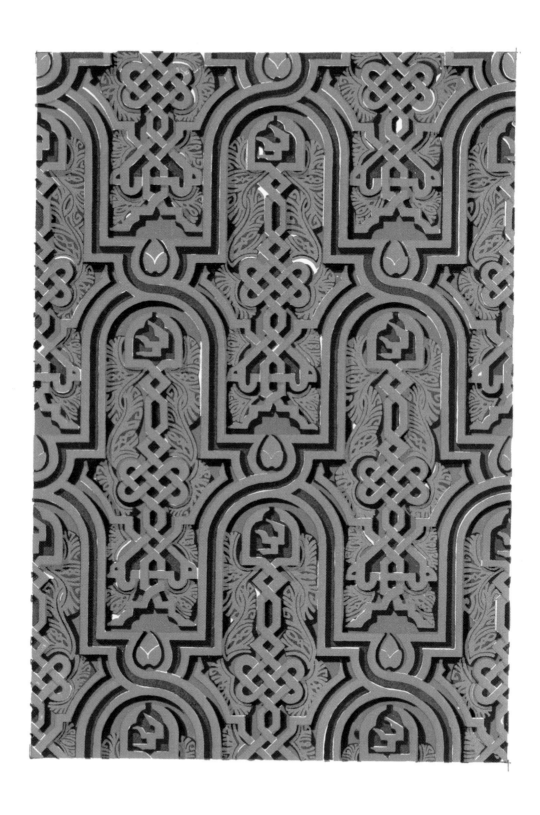

Ornaments on panels; Hall of the Ambassadors.

Ornaments on panels; Hall of the Ambassadors.

Ornaments on panels; Hall of the Ambassadors.

Details of the woodwork of the door to the Hall of the Abencerrages.

Frieze in the upper chamber; House of Sanchez.

60

Cornice at springing of arches; windows of the Hall of the Ambassadors.

From the entrance to the divan; Hall of the Two Sisters.

From the center arch of the Court of the Lions.

Spandrels of arches.

62

Spandrels of arches; Hall of Justice.

63

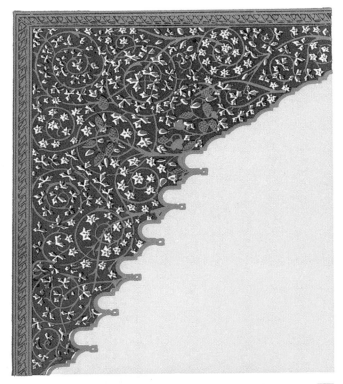

From the entrance to the Court of the Fish
Pond from the Hall of the Bark.

From the entrance to the Court of the Lions from
the Court of the Fish Pond.

Spandrels of arches.

Mosaics from the Hall of the Ambassadors; Hall of the Two Sisters and Hall of Justice.

65

Ornaments on the walls of the Hall of the Ambassadors.

Panels on walls; Tower of the Captive.

Plaster ornaments, used as upright and horizontal bands enclosing panels on the walls.

Mosaics from the Hall of the Ambassadors, Hall of the Two Sisters,
Hall of Justice, and Court of the Fish Pond.

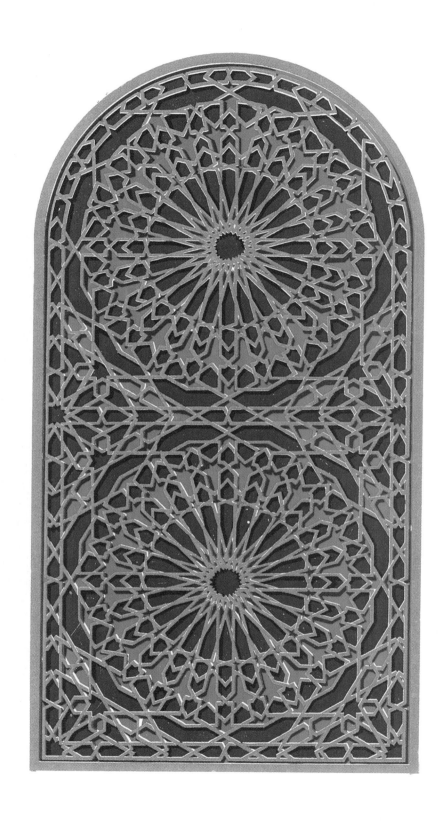

Blank window; Hall of the Bark.

Paneling of the center recess; Hall of the Ambassadors.

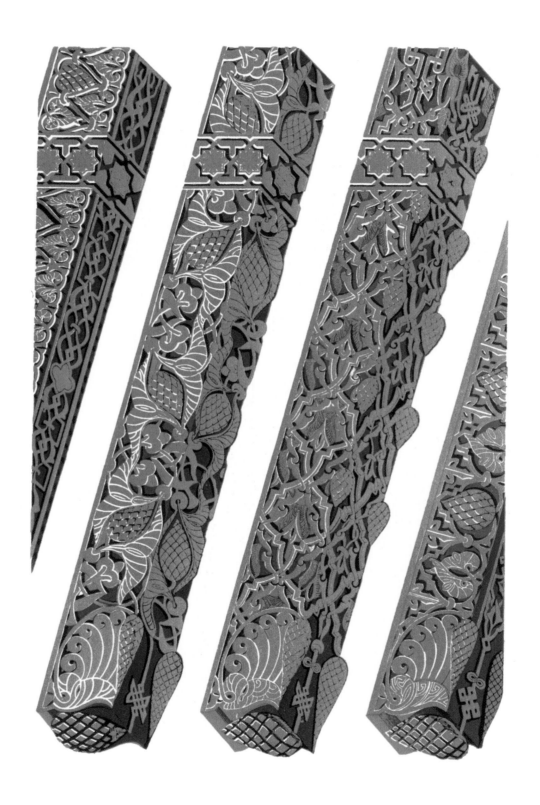

Rafters of a roof over a doorway now destroyed beneath the Tocador de la Reyna.

Band at springing of arch at the entrance of the Hall of the Two Sisters from the Court of Lions.

Part of ceiling of the portico of the Court of the Fish Pond.

Blank window; Hall of the Bark.

Ornaments on the walls; House of Sanchez.